Contents

Preface		1
1	Is there a vision?	2
2	Do we have the right skills for change?	6
3	How are we motivated?	10
4	Do we have the right technical skills?	14
5	Do we have enough resources?	18
6	Do we have the right organisation for change?	22
7	Do we have the right action plan?	26
8	Can we deal with objections?	29
9	Have we managed expectations?	33
10	What will the new environment be like?	37
About the Author		40
Contacts		41

©2013 Informita Limited. All rights reserved.

Preface

There are many change management books out there that tend to be too long, have too much theory and have ideas that are not easy to implement. This booklet takes a different approach. I have reviewed my 20 years of experience of change management and tried to boil it down to ten practical things that will help anyone to manage a programme of change. I have seen programmes where the change management side was ignored and therefore the programme failed. Equally, I have seen psychologists let loose on an unsuspecting organisation with very mixed reviews. While change is an emotive subject, people in a commercial organisation are rarely concerned with whether they were asked how they "feel" about the upcoming change. They want hard facts about how they will be affected. One gentleman once pulled me aside and asked me straight: "My life is about me, my wife and my kids. Are you here to mess that up or will you help?" The good news was that it was not going to be messed up. But it did highlight that people need to feel in control of events. In this booklet I will attempt to lay out some practical steps that can be taken, without any need for psychological jargon, in the real workplace that will not only help to make change happen but create an environment where change is sought out and therefore will perpetuate itself.

I will apologise in advance where I have failed in that aim and I hope you find the content useful to your change role.

1 Is there a vision?

One of the prime responsibilities of leaders is to provide a vision to the organisation of the changes required to make the organisation better or to focus the organisation on staying ahead of the competition. But rarely are leaders called visionary and this leads to some very predictable problems. It is not enough for leaders to seek change in the organisation but they must also map out what that change will mean. That is vitally important to the members of the organisation. At some stage the design of any change gets too detailed for the leader to know every nook and cranny. It is therefore necessary that the people managing that detail understand what their leader wants so that they take actions that are in line with the leader's vision.

This sounds very basic but is vitally important to the success of any change programme. At a nuclear services provider it was decided that all ERP platforms should be amalgamated onto one single and improved system. The constituent parts of the organisation had very different views of what an improved system would look like, but the vision described by senior management only asked for a single improved system without specifying the characteristics or purpose of that improved system. The programme ran into the sand after few months since no-one could agree on what the new system would look like and sufficient direction had not been given from above. Everyone at every level could see that the project was failing but the disagreement continued while senior management were unable to describe a realistic vision to the team. Eventually it was decided to hire an external programme director who had the experience and personality to get the programme done. He listened to the description of the original vision and then added the phrase "fit for purpose". So it didn't matter that they were not going to create the best system ever, but it was sufficient that they would create a single ERP platform that would be easily better than the systems that preceded it, but it only had to pass a "fit for purpose" test. The result was a system that did work, but whose parameters were driven by project deadlines and not the long term business need.

On the other hand, when senior management do have a clear vision for the business and this is communicated well then it is much easier for middle managers and process designers to interpret this vision into change that fits with the businesses' longer term goals. At one IT company that was mainly involved as a reseller of electronics, they bought a much bigger business that was more focused on the delivery and maintenance of complex IT programmes and IT outsourcing. They realised that the company they had acquired was very poor at tracking profitability by project and they knew they had to improve their own systems quickly to be able to deal with the project accounting aspects of these complex programmes. Anyone familiar with running an IT projects business knows that technical or financial problems caused by poor project and cost management can mean huge losses. There was an imperative to get these things right. So the vision from management was to have a single ERP platform that would have simple processes, allow for effective project management and give visibility to projects' financial status at any given point in time. When the design team got to their task they were able to quickly design the system with the necessary capabilities including effective project control processes. This shortened the timescale of the total project and delivered a system that was not just "fit for purpose", but capable of delivering the cost synergies that were the prime logic for the two organisations coming together in the first place.

But there are many organisations where their leaders do not understand the importance of vision. That isn't a problem as long as those leaders recognise their deficiency and employ someone with the necessary skills. But very often pride gets in the way of better judgement. Just because you have a particular title does not automatically mean that you are competent at your job. For those of you are unfamiliar, this is called The Peter Principle and states that "Employees tend to rise to their level of incompetence", i.e. employees are promoted to the next rank by doing their previous job very well. Eventually they will be promoted to a job that they are incapable of doing well. The real problem can be what happens next. An individual will either surround themselves with competent people to disguise their own incompetence or will continue with the delusion that they remain competent. The later will make some terrible mistake and get fired. The former is very likely to continue to retirement with a simple strategy of not taking risks in order to avoid mistakes at all costs.

But many organisations are very slow to weed out these leaders. As a result the organisation can stagnate and even fall on its sword completely. In many cases these leaders genuinely believe they are great leaders of change because their immediate reports are very effective at reinforcing the myth. It would be a brave person who would tell his or her boss that they believe their boss could do better and that is why it doesn't happen that often. And even when it does happen most bosses quickly discount the opinions of those with whom they disagree.

Achieving Change

The biggest modern barrier to leadership that provides real vision is the short-term culture that has many businesses trapped. From an individual leader's perspective there is no point having the best vision for change for the long term when you may be fired for having a few quarters of poor numbers. So the short term goals are prioritised making it more difficult to create the necessary mental space to think about how the business should develop and the plans that need to be in place to make that change happen.

2 Do we have the right skills for change?

Many programmes fail because the team lack the softer skills required to enable change to happen effectively. The key change management skills required are a clear understanding of organisational readiness, making sure that general communications are tailored to answer the specific concerns of the organisation, effective and frequent communication to smaller groups and clearly demonstrating that as events unfold that lessons are being learned and that the new environment will be better.

Trying to implement change without any of these factors being in play is disturbingly common and usually shows that the skills of the change team are overly focused on technical success or that the leadership of the change team lack these necessary skills. At a UK based IT distribution firm that had just taken over and Italian IT projects firm this is exactly what happened. The team had previously implemented SAP and rolled it out successfully to four other European affiliates. So when the acquisition came along they were very confident that they would take their ERP template and impose it on the acquired businesses and all would be well. The slogan of the company had been "speed over accuracy", i.e. make change happen quickly and if it's not perfect then we can go back later and fix it later. This philosophy had built up based on the fear that if change did not happen quickly, the solution being implemented might be obsolete by the time it was up and running. The acquired business was much larger, more complex and had a very different culture to the acquiring firm. But none of these vital differences were understood before a very quick ERP go live in the first pilot. Needless to say the pilot was a complete disaster. The operations of the acquired business stopped for over 3 weeks. It was impossible to process a purchase order, deal with purchase invoices correctly or to issue customer invoices. The change team had not listened to any of the concerns since they believed that they had a proven process template and they had been arrogant enough to think that because they were the acquirer their business model was always superior to that of the acquired.

On the technical side, they had seen any input that might have improved the process template as resistance to be ignored. In the acquired business, products would be purchased that would be specific to a client project. So to process a supplier invoice effectively there needed to be a project code. Project team members would need to allocate their time to each customer project, so a time allocation process was required. To produce a customer bill it was necessary to allocate the right costs and time allocations to customer projects and have an effective process for customers to sign off the relevant work done and costs incurred.

On the softer side, the team had misunderstood silence for compliance. They had just taken over a much larger organisation where many people were worried about job security. There was no communication strategy to tell people what the change might look like. There was no opportunity for most people to provide feedback on the proposed process changes and there was very little training given since the change team believed that using the new system was very intuitive – which it wasn't. When the system was shown not to work in the new environment a series of clunky spreadsheet driven workarounds were devised to get the business back to basic operations.

Senior management were horrified by what had happened and they did understand that a radically different approach was required. As a first priority the first pilot would need to be fixed. It took several more months for a revamped technical team to fix the first pilot to a point where these workarounds were no longer required. Secondly, there would have to be a much more structured approach to how the new process template was developed, communicated, signed-off by the local affiliates and effectively tested by end users. Processes were written down in a format that all end users could easily understand. Service level agreements were drafted at a process operator level so that individuals understood what was expected of them and what they should expect of their colleagues. Training formats were devised where end users would learn about the physical process and the ERP tasks all in the same session. All this was tested with the first and second pilot organisations to ensure that processes and tasks were properly understood and would actually work. On the softer side a specific change management team was created to help understand people's concerns and anxieties and to devise an effective communications strategy. That did not mean people suddenly vented all their frustrations, but it did create a process by which people could feed back their concerns and made it much more likely that their managers would not only listen to these concerns but feed them up the line. Communications were devised to answer some very basic questions like why was a new system required and what improvements were expected from this new process environment. Smaller groups were brought together to discuss individual issues on a purely confidential basis. This helped senior management to understand the level of anxiety that existed in the business and what issues they needed to focus on in order to address those anxieties. Newsletters were issued that communicated the progress that was being made and how the various forms of input had contributed to the change programme in a positive way.

All of this was then framed within a complete roll-out methodology focused on what we called "process testing". After the second pilot went live successfully, there were still eight more roll-outs across Europe that needed to be completed in the following nine months. Process testing was an opportunity for each affiliate to test each business process at the operator level of detail and their opportunity to sign off on the model or to provide input to make those processes more robust. All the subsequent roll-outs were completed to time and budget with a satisfied business user community.

3 How are we motivated?

Whenever any change programme is initiated there are always those people who are enthusiastic early adopters of change. These are the same people that go out and buy the latest gadget, even though the reviews say that it will be full of bugs and that you would be much wiser to wait for the second release. Equally there are those people who will always be against any kind of change, even when the benefits of such change are completely obvious. But in reality the vast majority of people don't really care about change as long as they are not adversely affected and that they have backed the winner.

Most people's lives are not based around their careers, but are based around their families and their relative well being. So the fact that you want to restructure the company, create a shared service, outsource, implement a new system or change the way the company's procedures operate is of no interest as long as two things are not threatened – their level of income and their security of employment. Most people work to live, i.e. to ensure that they and their families live in a state of relative comfort. They do not want to be the CEO of the company; they don't have a career plan and equally they don't want to become famous for leading the revolution against management. But they do not want to be seen to have backed a lost argument. So it should be fully expected that when the new programme is announced that most people will not respond in any demonstrable way. They will wait to see how things progress and will only become a follower when they see success being delivered.

Many companies will try to incentivise people with financial bonuses based on achieving set milestones. There is no doubt that this will have a short term positive effect on results, but study after study ever since Maslow has shown that money on its own is not an effective or sustainable long term motivator. It is very tempting to offer someone a pay rise to stop them from leaving the organisation, but the truth is that once someone has decided to resign their heart is no longer in the project or the mission. Emotionally they have moved on so even if they accept the pay rise you have only postponed the evil day.

And the more an individual is paid the more true this becomes. Most people can remember a time when they got their monthly pay cheque and then had to ration out payments, prioritising those companies that would take the roof off your head versus those who would not. If you are in this situation and your boss offers you a 10% pay rise then it's probably going to be very significant to you. On the other hand if you have passed the point where you have to worry about paying the bills every month that same 10% pay rise is less likely to make a significant impact on your lifestyle. This increases the likelihood that more of your judgements will be influenced by non-monetary factors like how much you enjoy your job or how your job enables you to live the lifestyle that you want or whether you consider your job to be the pinnacle of your career or a mere stepping stone to that goal. Bosses often get this wrong and end up overpaying people to do jobs that they eventually leave anyway. This is not to discount money as a motivator, but it is unlikely to be completely effective unless there are other levers at play.

If you speak to most people who have been involved in a successful change programme they will acknowledge that there may have been long hours involved, lots of tense discussions and even a few arguments but they usually enjoyed the whole process and got a massive kick out of succeeding. There are even some people who don't want to go back to the normal routine after the project is complete and want more of the change drug. There are now many people out there who have made a profession out of leading these types of change programmes without having any desire to do line roles or to end up as the boss of an entire company.

There will always be those who are ambitious for promotion and titles. Money is not their primary motivator. They will see a change programme as an opportunity to shine in front of others. Just like the majority of people mentioned earlier, they may not care about the goals of the programme but they fully understand how their star could rise as a result of the programme being successful and them being associated with that success.

And lastly there are those out there who simply want to do the right thing. This is usually a very small minority who will continue to do what they believe is best without any reward at all. These are the type of people who are often fantastic in either public service or charitable situations. They don't care about reward or glamour. As a result, in the general business world, these people can be passed over for promotions and pay rises since employers don't feel under pressure to keep these people. They are just taken for granted. This is a great shame since these individuals are most likely to be recognised as role models. So mistreating role models does not do much to encourage others to emulate their behaviour.

Since there are many different types of people in the organisation with many different personal drivers it would not be correct to assume that one framework of motivation will drive all individuals toward the organisational goal. It is incumbent on managers to recognise the way individuals can be motivated and to extract the best performance from all the team. Incentivisation is not always about money and does not always have a linear relationship with the scale of achievement. In one environment operators were given low value shopping vouchers for achieving financial targets. That scheme was very successful since it tapped in to people's pride in winning something. There are other cases of very well paid people feeling very de-motivated because they lack a sense of achievement or purpose. So one size does not fit all and there is no magical formula for managers to understand who fits in the correct box. But the more experienced and emotionally aware managers will be much better at identifying the various traits and playing to the correct strengths.

4 Do we have the right technical skills?

So far we have focused on some of the softer skills required to create effective change, but there is no point in embarking on a serious change programme unless the technical capability exists to get tasks completed to a sufficient level of competency.

The best example in everyday life is buying a house. First you will talk to a realtor or estate agent to show you a selection of properties that might be of interest. When you find the right property you will need a lawyer to manage the paperwork and a financial advisor to get you the best mortgage deal. You will then need to get the house insured. If you then embark on some remodelling you will need an architect and a competent builder with the right variation of skills that can make everything happen. It would be a very rare thing indeed for one individual to do all these things themselves since most of us would not be competent. We need the right specialists or else our project could turn into an expensive money pit.

And it's similar in the business world. A very good example would be the implementation of a new ERP system. It would be pretty obvious that you would need a group of technical specialists that are familiar with that ERP system and how it can be configured to suit the business. Many have also learned to their cost that a team of internal business specialists will also be required to help the external ERP specialists to understand the business properly so that the right configuration options are chosen. Will that mean that there will be major changes to operational processes such as how we input a sales order from a customer? Then we may need to hire specialist trainers and people with softer change management skills to ensure that operators understand the change that is coming down the road and are not anxious about the fact that things will be done differently. Are we going to be letting people go as a result of the changes that get implemented? We may need some human resource specialists who understand how employees need to be legally consulted about the forthcoming changes and what steps must be taken before making people redundant. And then all these people will need to be co-ordinated to ensure they are all doing the rights things in the right sequence at the right time. That's an awful lot to get right.

This is why many companies will employ an external systems integrator who will have most of these skills under one umbrella. And some do, but unfortunately many don't. For example many system integrators are very technically focused and are not well equipped in the softer skills of communication and training. The Big Four will have a distinct advantage in this area as long as you understand that you will get some experts and lots of academy members who are still learning their trade. And if you go for the umbrella solution you will pay the highest price for implementation. But you do mitigate the risk of not getting all the skills at the right level across the programme.

A vital question can be whether you recognise a real expert or not. Most of us have to rely on the quality of résumés and our own instinct for recognising the good people from the bad. If we go back to the house example, we employ lawyers, surveyors and architects since they all have important jobs to do and we trust their expertise since they have proven qualifications to do the job. But often that is not the case in change programmes. While there may be many programmes of certification they are no guarantee of success. For example, someone having a

Prince2 qualification does not make them a good project manager. It only tells you that they have a qualification that they paid for and they should be able to remember the elements of technical project management.

It is an unfortunate fact that most companies only find out afterwards how expert the experts really were. Several years ago when working at a major aerospace client we asked what the standard payment term was for their suppliers. The answer was 60 days after the month of purchase. So you should get an average 75 days of credit on these invoices. But we were puzzled that the due dates on these invoices were all 60 days after the date of purchase while the actual payment dates were slightly short of the 75 days average. After some investigation we found that when implementing SAP that their system integrator had told them that automatic configuration of such a term was impossible. The client had no reason to believe that this was not true and so had implemented a series of workarounds that meant rather than running a single payment run every week they ran fourteen separate payment runs with each tweaking invoice receipt date parameters to approximate the correct payment term. It was a very clever workaround but was completely unnecessary. Anyone who knows SAP will tell you that you simply need to flag one check-box in one table to make all this possible. But it does display the danger of trusting someone to be an expert in their subject when they clearly were not. What is worse in this case the system integrator encouraged the client to fit into a suboptimal process to cover their own technical incompetence on this point.

That might seem like a very narrow point but the quality of implementation will be heavily dependent on the level of expertise of the implementer. This is where external quality audits or expert user groups can be very beneficial so that clients can cross reference their experiences in order to get a better implementation result. But many continue not to make such checks and live with the consequences for a very long time.

5 Do we have enough resources?

In a large organisation it is fairly safe to say that the more resources allocated to a particular issue or project then the more likely it is that you will make progress on that issue. But this can also create problems. If one issue is prioritised over everything else then it is likely that all the other issues will suffer through a lack of focus and resources. The traditional answer in such cases is that you should hire outside resources to supplement your current resource pool so that all the major issues can be dealt with in an adequate fashion. But even then bottlenecks are created. In many cases there will be a few key individuals that all the projects need to reference so that they understand the background to the issues at hand and use the experience of those key individuals to come to the right conclusions more quickly.

The danger in such cases is that the urgency to complete the programme overtakes all other requirements and increases the likelihood that you get outcomes that are "fit for purpose" rather than the optimal solution for that business. If you have used external consultants it becomes more likely that there will be very little knowledge transfer during the life of the programme. Once the external consultants have done their job they leave and the experience goes with them. This is most common with technology implementations. At one client they had brought in external expertise to implement a state of the art credit and collections system. While the technical implementation went extremely well the financial results post implementation were a disappointment. On further investigation it was found that much of the functionality that was available was not being used since the key individuals who were also key users had been inadequately trained and had not been part of the implementation process. At another client the external consultants did a flawless technical job of implementing supplier catalogues. Two years after the implementation was completed not a single supplier catalogue had gone live due to the lack of properly qualified and experienced procurement professionals within the client who could have set up the commercial side of the process.

This has become a particular problem with regard to low cost country outsourcing. Although the goals of the outsourcing programme may have been achieved, i.e. reduce back office cost, a lot of experienced personnel are lost from the parent organisation as a result of the process. The theory is supposed to be that the outsourcer's people will work in close partnership with the client organisation to the point where this deep experience is properly replaced. In practice staff turnover rates in these outsourcing companies is very high. One reason for this is that many people employed to do process operator roles are grossly under-employed. For example, it is very common that people who work in shared service centres and outsourcer operations in Central and Eastern Europe will speak multiple European languages and probably have a master's degree. But many of these people will start jobs, such as invoice clerks, doing extremely basic administration roles. So the work is not fulfilling to people who are more than intellectually capable. Secondly, many of these shared service centres are based in purpose built office parks that are often completely populated by other shared service centres doing almost exactly the same functions. So anyone with any experience at all will try to get a job for better money and they only have to move across the street. In some parts of India they reckon that wage inflation is in excess of 20% in these types of office parks since it is so easy for people to change job. Thirdly, these jobs offer a very limited career path. While it may be very possible to advance yourself within the shared service structure, it is usually not possible to transfer to other functions in the parent/client organisation that could provide a path of advancement to these well qualified people. So the only way of having a career is to leave for another company. There are of course the exceptions but there are not many. This means that the resource capability of the organisation is reduced in the long term and means it is more likely that other external resources will be required to successfully complete future change programmes accentuating the risk that future knowledge transfer will fail.

In smaller organisations the problem of resource capability is almost always compounded by the bottlenecks created by having only a small number of sufficiently capable personnel and by the lack of financial resource available to employ expensive third party consultants. It can also be a major cause of organisational growing pains: being big enough that systems and processes need to become more advanced in order to keep a growing business under control, but at the same time being too small to avoid those personnel bottlenecks and afford external assistance. This is why there are very few organisations in the modern world who have survived all the way from being a small start-up to being a corporate giant. Many decide that it is easier to cash in their chips and pool in with a larger operator who has already overcome these restraints. But there are those who succeed in passing that barrier and they tend to be extremely innovative companies not just because of the products they make or the services they deliver, but also in the way their business operates. Obvious examples in the digital world are Apple, Google, Facebook and Twitter. But there examples in the non-digital world too like Dyson and South

West Airlines of companies built around a business operating model or invention that succeeds at every stage of corporate growth.

So it is better to ask if you have the optimal number of resources for your programme rather than enough. Too many is just as bad as too little. And it is always important to ensure that the right resources will be in place after the programme is complete so that the benefits of change can be sustained and even bettered in future years.

6 Do we have the right organisation for change?

There are two aspects that need to be correctly diagnosed before building your project organisation. The first is to understand the nature of the organisation you are trying to change and then the shape and style of the project organisation will follow.

Several years ago while working at a major US timber products organisation one of their executives told me: "Around here the generals give the orders and the troops will march!" Although an organisation of many thousands of people spread over many divisions, the command structure of the organisation was completely centralised. When senior management gave orders execution would be swift. So it was necessary to assemble a large team that could deploy in several divisions simultaneously so that when the "troops" started marching they had the right tools and training to implement the desired changes that were mandated.

Contrast that with a global pharmaceutical major with affiliates in more than 160 countries across the globe. The desire was to improve accounts receivable performance. But in an intelligent organisation where sales, marketing and customer relations are governed independently at the affiliate level and not the centre, there was no point deploying a large team since the tools largely existed already. What they were missing was a global policy on how they would deal with customer credit issues across the organisation. A small team was put together to construct a document that would be agreeable to all the affiliates and would work through various regional management teams to gain agreement on the policy document.

In consensus driven organisations a different approach may be required. Very often the skills to get things done exist in the organisation already. The difficulty can be persuading all the relevant stakeholders not just of the need for action but the form that action should take. This again does not mean that you require a large team to get things done, but it will mean that you will need someone who is skilled at facilitating between the parties to help them understand that they have a common goal and they need to work together to deliver change.

The intelligent organisation is much more capable at debating every possible scenario and thus slowing down progress, and is also capable of choosing solutions that are massively over-specified. For example, at a Dutch plastics company that had just merged with another plastics company, we were in the process of creating a gap analysis between the respective organisations' business processes. On one particular day the subject was outbound logistics. The first company sent their team of 5 people who managed the process and the second sent one guy who did everything for them. The first company had a system that was completely automated. Even when a logistics provider informed them that they were unable to transport a particular load the route was automatically sent out for e-auction. Everyone agreed that this was one of the most advanced solutions we had ever seen and the team from the first company were very proud of their achievement. The guy from the second company then described his process as picking up the phone and calling companies to get the best deals and provide routing instructions. The companies were roughly of equivalent size, but one solution was massively over elaborate.

You could argue that the other solution was too simplistic. But it does show that the way an organisation thinks will evidence itself in the complexity of their structures and processes.

Any project organisation must have the right mix of technical and soft skills and be organised in a fashion that not only allows the various specialists to deliver results to the organisation in general but also allows the project team to work effectively together. This can be particularly true for ERP implementations where there may be a wide community of specialists who are part of the total team but who do not necessarily understand each others' specialties. The scramble for project resources will demand that three things must be in place; a clear project methodology, clear and regular lines of communication and clear lines of authority within the team.

Especially in large teams there is a need to develop a team methodology so each team member understands their role and how that role interacts with all the others in the team. There is no set template for a project methodology since it will vary by organisation and by the nature of the change programme. But without it will be very difficult to bring the various specialists out of their respective foxholes and shape them into a team with a single purpose and goal. This will then allow many micro decisions to be made by team members themselves since they will have a proper understanding of the context of their individual actions.

The need for communication can never be understated. In a large team there will be many things going on at once and there is a constant need for co-ordination of activities. But many programmes get bogged down in communication. Conference calls can go on for hours without making any decisions and the list of problems can be seen to grow longer and escalate. Team communications should be regular and brief. Discussions should be limited to tasks completed, tasks scheduled and risks and issues. Each of these meetings will need an effective chair to ensure that all team members have a voice and that discussions are constructive. This format saves a lot of time and ensures that progress is always being driven on. To be genuinely effective a good project leader will be required.

Large projects usually have a community of intelligent and strong personalities. The strong project leader is required to ensure that the team works together and that any resource disputes are resolved constructively. This is not always an easy process. The same person must also make sure that all those strong talented people stay on board with the programme and demonstrate the progress of the team.

7 Do we have the right action plan?

On one of my first assignments as a consultant my manager told me to draft a project plan, to print it out and stick it on the wall of our office. Being new to the game, I asked how we could put a viable plan together on our first day on site given we didn't know anything about the client, their issues or the kind of things we would need to do over the following seven weeks that would help matters improve. He swiftly explained to me that all that didn't matter straight away. He wanted a plan on the wall so that if the client walked into the room, they would see that plan on the wall and they would have the automatic impression that we knew what we were doing. Clearly this was a very cynical set of instructions that I was given, but the odd thing was that he was completely correct. Of course the plan was updated on a regular basis afterwards, but on many occasions the client would enter the room, look at the plan and occasionally offer some comments and questions. The client got comfort from knowing there was a plan and that progress was being made. But that is only one purpose of having a plan.

Plans will vary in their level of detail and style. In the case above the client only wanted a very simple high level plan. In the Anglo-Saxon world this can be common since many people think they will intuitively understand the detail. Many times this turns out not to be the case and this increases the need for project management to ensure that everyone is singing from the same hymn sheet. But there are cases where such a plan is doomed to failure.

On my first assignment in Scandinavia, we had a plan that had already been successfully rolled out in the UK, France, Germany,

Switzerland, Belgium and the Netherlands. As a team we were very confident in our ability to deliver this plan. So we then found it extremely frustrating to have everyone in Copenhagen asking lots of detailed questions about every line in the plan. We had completely misunderstood the mood. We thought that the locals were trying to slow us down with all these detailed questions. But from their perspective if they were to operate as an effective team they needed to understand every detail as a team before they could begin implementation. Our frustration continued until they decided as a group that they all understood the plan, their individual part of the plan and that the plan was viable. What ensued was the fastest implementation of a plan that I have ever seen that went off without any glitches at all. I was truly impressed and learned a big cultural lesson. Just because the previous plan had worked successfully several times did not mean it would work in all places and that the nature and style of that plan had to reflect the local culture of how things got done. Usually what will cause personal frustration in these situations is your own lack of understanding of that local culture, not the culture itself.

Planning documentation might be boring to do, but it is essential to a programme's success. Sponsors and stakeholders need to see that progress is being made and the team itself requires co-ordination. But remember that a good project planner is not always a good project manager. While working at a major UK utility company that was in the middle of a total company transformation programme a joke went around about their chief project planner to the effect that because of him the project might not be delivered on time but at least they would know exactly why.

Achieving Change

A really good project planner will have the ability to review and understand a whole series of seemingly disparate plans from numerous disciplines and by trying to integrate those plans can create the critical path for programme success. Equally the same planner will understand when elements of the plan do not integrate properly and then something will have to change. Each element of the team will need to understand the problem and suggest viable changes, which again the planner has the job of attempting to integrate and ensure that timescales and resources will work within the project timescales. Without using someone with these skills it is very likely that at some point the project will stop due to an unforeseen problem and therefore a critical path will be broken.

8 Can we deal with objections?

Every change programme will need to deal with objections of some kind but two things are essential when dealing with objections: sponsorship and technique. Without the right sponsorship you will not have the authority to deal with any objections. Without the right technique you are likely to deal with objections in an unconstructive manner.

Concerns are always valid and must be dealt with properly. Concerns are not usually about hostility to the programme but are driven by personal anxiety and the fear of change. This is often the case when objection statements are general in nature and lack specificity. Objections can be a symptom of lack of understanding or lack of experience about the programme and its impact. Objections are an opportunity to bring the individual closer emotionally to the path of change by taking the opportunity to communicate directly and interactively about the nature of the programme. Dealt with properly, real objections are not barriers to change. In fact objections are necessary as part of any constructive feedback. How else will issues and flaws be ironed out ahead of implementation?

Once the nature of any objections are understood you will need to find out the criteria that will allow change to happen through uncovering cultural information from stakeholders, i.e. how do we get things done around here? If concerns are ignored or detected late in the programme the results can be disastrous. So concerns and objections need to be detected early in the process of change. If done properly detection of any potential resistance can be used to accelerate change.

Achieving Change

To be a successful change agent you are expected to be a believer at all times. Persistence is a requirement. There is never a time to give up. You will almost certainly meet resistance of some kind during the programme. The trick is that when you expect resistance, you will be ready when it arrives. Your success will be based on your perceived value to the stakeholders. Perceived value will be gained through your technical knowledge about the problem, your ability to convey the issues in an amicable fashion and your ability to sense the emotional state of the stakeholder. If you are not good at change management then expect lots of arguments and disagreement and you will need to constantly escalate issues to the Steering Committee for resolution.

It is necessary to find friends and discount objections quickly. In any case there are the 10% of early adopters. They seek change for its own sake. They will be full of enthusiasm for the programme on the first day but they will get bored with the project once the next issue comes along. There will always be the 30% who do not want change. Change makes them anxious as it may threaten their position. They view change as unnecessary or even dangerous and they will have a list of objections that must be exhausted quickly. The remaining 60% want to back the winner. They are more interested in their personal progress than the issue at hand. They must be convinced in order to embed the desired change but vitally they are the people who will sustain the change.

Objection statements can be grouped as moral, emotional or factual. Examples of moral objections might be the belief that the programme approach is too aggressive or that it might be unfair to a customer, supplier or employee. As a change agent it is your responsibility to point out why the change is fair and is not aggressive. It is always good to use comparisons with other companies who have done something similar and successfully. Emotional objections are evidenced by the fear of losing status or position and the fear of failure. Words may not be enough to overcome these types of objections. At one client a lady became physically sick at the thought of doing her job differently. She was completely capable but equally full of anxiety. So we struck a deal with her. We put one of our team side by side with her in the department. He would do her job in the new way under her supervision and she promised that if she saw it was working she would try the new way of working. After three days she accepted the new way of working and was actually very good. But that proof was required before she could move forward. The final type of objection is factual. Examples of factual objections would be that your analysis is wrong, your methodology is wrong or that what you are trying to achieve is impossible. If you believe that your analysis is correct, never be afraid to share that analysis with the person voicing the objection. That will help them to understand why you came to your conclusion. Equally if you have made a mistake in your analysis, but the general direction of the results is the same then making that mistake might be a good way of bringing the objector on board with the programme. If the objection is about methodology or viability, you must be able to demonstrate where this action has been taken before and how it succeeded. Case studies can be very useful to demonstrate such a case and the fuller they are with facts and figures the better.

The greatest objection you will ever hear is the one the "we are different". We can be different because of country, language, culture, business model, customer type, manufacturing process, the colour of your hair, your taste in music, where you went to school and so on and so forth. The potential list here is endless, but here is a simple reply. More than 99% of all human genes are identical in all people. So we are not exactly the same and we should take account of those differences properly and sensitively, but we should also recognise how similar we are and celebrate that fact. Very often transplanting a methodology from one industry to another or from one function to another can be highly successful and that innovation might mean that the implementation of change has delivered a strategic advantage that no one else yet possesses.

Also recognise that opposition takes energy. If you can convince your objectors that you are on the right track and they use the same energy to support the programme you may have found yourself a very powerful friend.

9 Have we managed expectations?

Anyone in business will always tell you that it is always better to under-promise and over-deliver. And that statement is very true in change management. Exuberance will usually lead you to be over enthusiastic about the outcomes of a change programme. This is a natural reflection of your own self-belief but it needs to be tempered with a measure of realism. It is unlikely that the end result will be exactly the same as the design at the start. Compromises will be required in order to flex to the needs of the business and to bring key stakeholders on board with the programme. Experience tells you to take that natural exuberance and turn it down a few notches. This is a must even when you know that everything you are saying is absolutely true and within the realms of possibility. But most people will also believe that if something sounds too good to be true then it probably is too good to be true.

It is always necessary to be honest about the pain involved in any change programme. There is no change programme that is pain free. The best that can be hoped for is that the pain is managed and is not unexpected. There must be a clear strategy that admits that pain is on the horizon but that also is capable of preparing the organisation for painful events. And some types of pain will be more obvious than others. Sometimes redundancies might be required and the effect on individuals, their families and communities is fairly obvious. This kind of pain can be mitigated by retraining schemes for individuals or community support schemes for areas of high unemployment. But very often pain is much more subtle and much more irrational. The fact that we ask people to do something different can be very scary. But often individuals do not want to admit that to their peers and colleagues. Many years ago the organisation I worked for at the time had implemented a brand new accounting system which had a number of improved features for users and was much more efficient than the previous systems. One specific feature of the old system was that when cash was received by customers it was one lady's job to allocate the cash received to the correct customer invoices. In the new process it was the job of the cash collector to allocate the cash to the right invoice. It was a very simple process where the users just needed to check the right tickboxes on the customer account screen and the job was done. Three months after we went live we were doing a series of ad-hoc reports in the accounts receivable department and noticed the value of unallocated cash had skyrocketed. On further investigation we found that it was down to the fact that one collector was not allocating cash at all. When we asked to understand why he was not allocating the cash he admitted that he had not understood the training properly and was afraid to ask in case he looked foolish in front of his colleagues. This problem was very easily resolved but does show how emotionally delicate even the smallest change can be to the individual.

The other fact about most change programmes is that external events continue during the programme and have the capability of forcing the programme to change in a way that could not have been anticipated at the start. Examples would be business divisions being bought or sold causing a fundamental change to the programme plan or core process design. At one company they had started a tender process to undertake a major change programme, but cancelled the whole effort when it became apparent that customer demand patterns had changed in such a way that would have meant that the programme would have been entirely inappropriate in the new circumstances. At another client, we had just started the programme of building their European shared service centre when they were taken over by another corporation. We came into work on Monday morning to hear the news of the takeover and the programme had been scrapped by 3pm the same day.

But there are other circumstances that can be anticipated and planned for, even if they never happen. Economic circumstances will change; there will be some part of the organisation where the level of pain coming from the programme becomes too high; there will be additional cost pressures for the programme. It is always difficult to keep the costs for a large programme under control. It is inevitable that some expenditure will prove to be larger than originally planned and it is increasingly difficult to have buffers in the programme budget that will not be discovered and eliminated by the accountants. So every programme has to have an expectation that there will be cost pressures in the latter stages of the programme and have a pro-active prioritised plan to deal with those changes. That could be swapping out expensive resources for something more reasonable, the reduction of resource requirements or the elimination of programme activities. But this must be managed carefully so that the quality of the change programme is not undermined. For example the two areas that are usually affected by this kind of cost pressure in ERP programmes are user testing and user training. Cutting these excessively will directly affect the success of the programme but happens extremely frequently. It is inevitable that some part of the organisation will experience more pain than might have been anticipated and it is necessary to have a programme plan that is flexible enough to bend to accommodate that high level of pain or to have additional support resources to mitigate that pain. It is very common that programme plans lack this kind of flexibility or resource causing programmes to become increasingly unpopular throughout their implementation. Finally, economic factors will almost always change. If the change is favourable then there is not much to worry about, but if not it is paramount that the case for change is watertight. A weak business case for change can easily be undermined in these circumstances.

The final point about managing expectations is that there should be as few surprises as possible. But this will depend on an effective reporting regime that is simple, frequent, transparent and involve as much direct contact with stakeholders as possible. Have a simple weekly report. Mine are colour coded so that the stakeholder can skip to the important issues quickly. The report should be on one page. Most stakeholders are very busy people and do not have the time to read essays on progress. It is vital that the programme manager has at least one hour of face time with the project sponsor every week. Some call this the fireside chat, but could be lunch or meeting up for coffee. Sponsors have usually staked their reputation on the success of the programme, so you cannot afford to let them down or let them fall out of the communication loop. And a well informed sponsor will be in a much better position to defend the programme in the face of the concerns of other stakeholders. So over communication is never a bad thing.

10 What will the new environment be like?

It can be a big surprise to a lot of people but the completion of a single successful change programme is rarely the end of the process. The very greatest organisations seek out change. They understand that if they do not then some other company will take their mantle. That does not mean that they go for the latest jingoistic form of change, but they do constantly review what is going on in the outside world to see what might be suitable for them and drive them on to greater efficiency and effectiveness.

There are organisations that strive to be world class in everything they do. While this is a lofty aim at times it can be quite inappropriate. At a formula one racing team an inventory management specialist suggested that adding RFID chips to key car parts would help the team to understand what inventories were on the road during the racing season and reduce the number of stock outs that in some cases could affect race performance. The engineers then asked how much the RFID chips would weigh when added to the total car. Once they knew this weight they worked out that adding the chips would cost them one tenth of a second per lap and was therefore rejected. That might seem a very small performance difference to a more usual company, but to a formula one racing team that could be the difference between winning a race and coming second.

One lesson that formula one teams are brutally aware of is that your past reputation for winning is no guide to the future. Unless you are prepared for constant change, in potentially all areas, you can never hope to be the champion and it will be even less likely that you stay champions.

The same is true in business. Being capable of rapid change is a strategic advantage in a world of ever changing technologies, fashions and methodologies. Those who believe that everything is just fine the way things are will continue to be fine until they reach a point of crisis. Then they will find themselves in a position where they are not equipped for change from either a technical or cultural perspective. Such organisations have a habit of disappearing over the decades.

But those that recognise that change is never finished will prove to be far more agile when the inevitable crisis does happen either because they will have technically shielded themselves from the potentially adverse effects of unlucky circumstances or that they are culturally equipped to recognise and deal with the problem head on.

And change must also be dynamic. Just because you completed the best ever change programme is no reason to rest on your laurels. It is inevitable that customer requirements and competitive pressures will change over time. So even the best process needs to be monitored, compared with the opposition and tweaked so that it continues to outperform. Organisations who think like this are not afraid to understand their own frailties and work hard to seek them out and resolve theses weaknesses. In my career I have only come across one organisation that invited us to review their processes because they wanted to ensure that they were the very best they could be. They knew they were pretty good but they wanted to be sure that they were not being complacent. The same organisation did not view the subsequent findings and recommendation with dread, but were fully capable of objectively absorbing this new information and taking corrective action that would improve those processes on a sustained basis.

Compared to the vast majority of organisations these guys were very brave. The vast majority of executives try to hide from change and their organisations suffer as a result. That is not to say that an organisation that is conservative about risk taking cannot be a top performer but being conservative for its own sake is just as destructive to growth as being too head strong in your desire for change.

There are those who deliberately join more conservative organisations with the aim of leading them to a path of change. They understand the monumental size of their challenge, that they may not always be able to get what they want and that it is likely to take some time. There are very few business leaders that can be called truly transformational, but they are out there and should be a real inspiration those who have been charged with implementing change. So understand your possibilities, be realistic and aware of others and be driven by your vision.

About the Author

Brian Shanahan is the leader and founder of Informita. Informita was formed in 2012 to assist companies in the areas of working capital and procurement, focusing on analytics, implementation and advisory. We like to call ourselves change management specialists with a focus on working capital and procurement. But the techniques and nuances of change are the same no matter what your programme is about.

Before Informita, Brian spent 19 years in management consultancy, 5 years in financial accounting roles in the UK and 3 years in retail in Ireland. To date Brian has worked with over one hundred clients in 35 countries across 4 continents.

In the media, Brian has been quoted many times in the financial press in such publications as The Financial Times, CFO World, The Manufacturer, The Grocer, Finance Director, Euromoney, Accountancy Age, Financial i and The Evening Standard. Brian has also appeared on CNBC Europe's Power Lunch.

Contacts

If you would like more information about Informita please feel to contact us in the following ways:

Website: www.informita.com

Email: info@informita.com

Phone: +44-20-3286-4109

Twitter/Facebook: @informita

www.ingramcontent.com/pod-product-compliance
Lightning Source LLC
Chambersburg PA
CBHW070718180526
45167CB00004B/1529